Go and the Lord go with thee!

D1711916

"Go and the Lord go with thee!", were Rebecca Jones' words to Thomas Scattergood during his visit to her sick-bed in 1793, when the yellow fever was raging in Philadelphia. His mind had long been exercised with a concern to visit Friends and others in Great Britain and Ireland but he was not clear that the time was right. He had not shared his thoughts with anyone. Rebecca, almost too ill to speak, looked up at him and uttered these words. Thomas knew then that he had to go.

The cover photograph is by Bosse Karlberg of Malmö, Sweden, writer and photographer of art.

Go and the Lord go with thee!

Sue Glover

Sessions Book Trust
York, England

ISBN 1 85072 198 X

Published by the Sessions Book Trust

Printed in 11½ on 13 point Plantin Typeface
with New Berolina Script
from Author's Disk
by Sessions of York
The Ebor Press
York, England

CONTENTS

FOREWORD
by Rex Ambler

Friends used to travel a lot. It was part of their culture, part of the unique form of life they introduced to the world. They had, after all, rejected most forms of communication that were thought generally to be necessary in religion. They had no authorities to appeal to, no priests to interpret religious truth, no liturgies to act out the religious story. All truth had to be experienced inwardly. How then could it be conveyed from one to another? The answer Friends came up with was to speak and act as the experience of inward truth led you to do so. Your life could 'preach'. So could your words, if they came from deep within. Indeed, if you were moved to speak, you had to speak. It was part of your own growth and spiritual health to act on these 'leadings of the Spirit', whether you wanted to or not.

So Friends at the beginning found themselves often being led into situations they would never have consciously chosen for themselves. Some spoke to kings. Some travelled a great distance to speak to pashas and sultans about the light within them. Some travelled to the American colonies to speak to the Indians, or to encourage and guide Friends already settled in Meetings. In this rather unique way the movement grew and the community of Friends flourished.

In our own time we hear little of Friends 'travelling in the ministry'. Why is this? Sue Glover's little book answers that question, and suggests why it may be time to think of travelling again. In doing this she recovers something of the clarity and passion of early Friends. She gives us a clear sense of what led Friends over the years to give so much time and energy to communicating their experience. But she also focuses well on the present. She describes with some understanding the caution that holds Friends back today, arising from our individualism and our (justified) suspicion of authority and dogma. But we are also in a time of crisis, when our own identity as Quakers is increasingly uncertain. It is time to recall our beginnings and share with one another what we really experience and really believe in. And out of this sharing we may gain the courage and desire to communicate our truth to the wider world.

Sue's book is also a practical guide on travelling with this concern. She has travelled widely herself among Friends and she has learned from other Friends who have travelled and experimented with different kinds of ministry. Having just begun to do this myself I found her examples, stories and advice all very helpful. I think the book will be helpful to many other Friends. I hope it will also encourage Friends to consider whether they too may be led into this unusual, risky and much-needed work.

May 1997   REX AMBLER
                                             Birmingham

INTRODUCTION

Since becoming part of the Quaker family, in 1976, I have been fascinated by the concept of 'travelling in the ministry'. It appealed to my simple understanding of Jesus' instructions to his disciples to "go into the whole world and preach the gospel to every creature" (Mark 16.15). When I read George Fox's advice to *"Let all nations hear the word by sound or writing. Spare no place, spare not tongue nor pen, but be obedient to the Lord God and go through the world and be valiant for the truth upon earth....."*, it slotted easily into place.

Heeding this, early Friends trumpeted the word of the Lord throughout England and the colonies, pushing out the boundaries of the new Quaker movement in their enthusiasm to share their insights and convictions. Despite the hardships and pain, they were joyfully certain of their re-discovery of the simple, yet incredibly deep, challenges of Christ. Their lives were changed and, in their travels, they helped to change the lives of thousands of others. What a remarkable thing that was.

What was their message? What had those first pioneers of the Quaker movement discovered afresh? Perhaps to answer these questions we need to look again at what Fox meant by the light and the truth, to remind ourselves of the power of the Spirit which stirred them into travelling far and wide. Even after they had gone, when the message was muted and less strident, there remained the power of the Spirit, with the capacity to shape a life in harmony with the absolute demands of the Sermon on the Mount.

Over the years, understanding and perception of the nature and thrust of 'travelling in the ministry' seems to have become tangled up with corporate fears of authority, evangelising, preaching and proselytising. Dramatic changes in Christianity since the 1650's have led to today's Quaker 'identity crisis', which may mean that we have lost the vision of what we believe in so that we don't feel we have anything specific to share. Anxieties may thus overtake us when some Friends find

1

themselves called to travel and speak of their experiences of moral and spiritual growth, as early Friends did.

During the last three years of moving extensively amongst Quakers in Europe, Australia, Aotearoa/New Zealand and Latin America, I have come across the ups and downs of Friends trying to share their faith in a world which is very different from that of the first pioneers. In Europe, Quaker meetings are experiencing a significant drop in numbers. Many Friends are elderly and isolated. Outreach is difficult. In contrast, in parts of the world such as Africa and Latin America, Quakers are sure in their faith and enjoying growth. Here the question might be how to sustain and nurture their many newcomers.

I have discovered that some European yearly meetings are experimenting with new forms of 'travelling in the ministry'. However, in conversations with some of the Friends who are engaged in this work, it becomes clear that many questions need to be asked and answers sought. What is the nature of the work? What are the expectations? How should it best be carried out? Whom are we trying to reach? Why are we doing it? .... are only some. The provocative words of Edgar G. Dunstan, *"Have you anything to declare?"* (QF&P: 28.07), have become almost constant companions as I searched for answers which might help.

One of the aims of this book is to clarify what is meant by 'travelling in the ministry' for it seems that Friends have different ministries to offer and their own experiences to relate. Perhaps the modern equivalents are leading us to take new and vital initiatives in the task of sharing our Quaker message with those who are still seeking for a spiritual home, as well as with those who have already found acceptable ones. Although there are signs of stagnation in the spiritual life of our movement, there are also those of great potential. Continuing to be a challenge to the accepted ways and standards of today's world is a task that Quakers may not shrink from. Can 'travelling in the ministry' be one of the ways in which we can effectively make our witness to the 21st Century?

Turning to the practicalities of this book, I have arranged it into five parts. Part one identifies the kernel of the Quaker message and outlines the travelling ministry of George Fox and his contemporaries and looks at its gradual decline. Part two maps out the steps involved in recognising and acting upon a 'concern'. The third part examines present-day travelling under concern and draws upon personal experiences. Part four takes a panoramic view of the pastoral tradition and finally, part five attempts to weave together some of the strands and invites – even challenges – Friends to use their imaginations.

As part of the preparation for this exploration, I wrote an introductory article asking Friends to respond to a number of specific questions related to 'travelling in the ministry'. The article was sent to Quaker publications in Britain, France, Switzerland, Australia, Norway, Sweden, Germany, the Netherlands, USA, Africa, Ireland and Finland and was published in some of them. The number of responses was not overwhelming – seven in all – but those received were pertinent. Besides this, I wrote a letter to 30 or so Friends known for their 'travelling under concern' and included a questionnaire. Although I did not get much feedback from Quakers who had received visitors, about half those I contacted responded and thanks to them I have been able to tell a story which I hope will be thought provoking.

My thanks are especially due to my life partner Franco Perna and also to Beth Allen, Rex Ambler, Philip Austin, Irwin & Sylvia Barnes, Marianne Boelsma, Brian Bridge, David Gray, Peggy Heeks, Edward Hoare, Teresa Hobday, Bosse Karlberg, Susanne Kromberg, Charles G. Lamb, Michael Langford, Eva Pinthus, Juliet Prager, David Pulford, William Sessions, Thomas Taylor, Brenda Wall, Ursula Windsor and Lilamini Woolrych.

Sue Glover, Padenghe sul Garda, Italy, May 1997

1 GOING OUT

The first itinerant Quakers were engaged in "publishing truth", as they understood it. Like most English people of the 1600's they were rooted in the Bible. Its images, phraseology and teachings were second nature to them. In the new Quaker message, they found what they believed was its true meaning. What was this revolutionary message that gripped them and sent them scattering to all corners of the world to tell others about?

George Fox knew, experientially, that God dwelt in human hearts and not in consecrated buildings. He had a horror of those who made a living out of preaching, believing that it should be done out of love. Although he could quote scripture and verse, he looked upon the Bible as secondary to the teaching of the eternal Christ. Fox had discovered that "there is one, even Christ Jesus, which can speak to thy condition". Whilst accepting that he and others were imperfect, he believed that it was possible to learn the way to perfection through a perfect teacher who, for him, was God in Christ. But how?

Light and truth

In his paper entitled "Quaker Identity – anything goes?", Rex Ambler sees that for Fox, spirituality was a very practical discipline. The kernel of Fox's belief was, that to have real life, one must know the truth. This truth, needed to bring us to real life, is to be found within us. The light that shows the truth to us is the pure light of God. It may make its presence felt by a stirring unease about how we are living – for example, when we have wronged someone or told something which is not true. In paying attention to this, we can begin to see ourselves as we really are. Seeing ourselves for what we are and being deeply dissatisfied with what we see, means that we have within us some sense of purity and goodness and a knowledge of what we ultimately ought to be. Fox experienced that this light takes us out of ourselves so that we can look objectively and dispassionately and see ourselves from God's point of view.

Before we can have any sense of how we might be different, it is important to accept the truth about ourselves and the world in which we live. This is difficult and takes courage. By a process of waiting for guidance in silence and stillness, surrendering to the truth that we become aware of, we can come to accept the conflict and confusion as part of what we are, thus becoming aware of our undeveloped aspects, the untapped resources and the new possibilities.

Being less concerned to hide our own faults and failings and living according to the truth, we are freed to care for others. This caring becomes a 'witness' to the truth we have seen and our collective acts of caring become our 'testimonies' to it. We become sensitive to a 'leading' or 'concern' as to how precisely to care. Our faith is then expressed in how we live our lives.

For those who are uncomfortable with the term "God", Rex explains it as being an ultimate reality, free of false images and illusions, which is opened up for us by seeing ourselves as we really are. To believe in God in this sense is to live according to the truth we see and to trust that we are ultimately safe with it.

Convincement and witness

By 1647, 23 year old Fox had grown confident enough to share his exhilarating experience and illuminations with anyone who would listen. He travelled on foot and often alone, along muddy and isolated tracks, sleeping out under a hedge or haystack if he couldn't find an inn. At this time the total population of England was around 5 million and apart from London, Norwich and Bristol, hardly 10 towns had over 5,000. One could travel for miles without seeing a person or a house. Roads were of beaten earth, with brushwood or rough stones tossed into the holes and one either rode on horseback, in carts or walked, covering about

3 or 4 miles an hour. Beggars and thieves molested travellers along lonely stretches and sometimes beat them to death.....

Travelling and telling of what amounted to his re-discovery of the original Christian message, Fox convinced many and provided the foundation for lives of great value. He insisted that Christ 'was come to teach his people himself'. As Christ stood for what was eternally true, it followed that, as people learned more and came closer to him in devotion and service, they would find themselves in closer unity with each other and their conduct more reliable and consistent. The insights and experience he spoke of proved to have the potential and capacity for moral and spiritual growth, able to cope with a changing society and a world beyond. Realising for himself the profound truth of the Sermon on the Mount (Matthew 4:5-7:29), Fox saw no limits. He treated everyone alike, practised nonviolence and refused to swear an oath. He challenged the law, defended himself with genius at trials and witnessed to the truth at all times. His complete loyalty to the Lord meant being open to people of other faiths, for what mattered was whether they were truthful and compassionate, rejecting oppression and persecution. His primary interest was focused on the activities of people, preferring to speak outdoors or in the intimate surroundings of their homes.

Those changed by his thinking became ready to follow his example and leave home to undertake long and dangerous journeys around the country. They were not people specially appointed, set apart or ordained as ministers. They were ordinary folk, with a burning desire to share their new awareness, confident that their message was a simple truth about the nature of faith and humanity and sure that if others could be reached, they too would be convinced and their lives transformed. One could say that they had entered the kingdom of love and were walking in the way of truth.

The first generation of travelling speakers or "publishers of truth" numbered about 70 and included both men and women. If we add those who only worked locally, for a short time or as a companion to others, the number is greater. For them, the Quaker life was not complete without spreading the work of the Spirit to the world as a whole. They represented a radical and challenging emphasis within a generally accepted religious culture. By simple and direct ministry in the language of the day, and the experience of the power of silence in worship, they aimed to turn people to the light of Christ and the true centre within themselves.

Prepared for anything, they delivered their message at market crosses, in churches, private homes and anywhere people would assemble. Unstoppable, they endured beatings, duckings, insults and imprisonments. Their coming was often known about beforehand through the existing, patchy network and letters of introduction carried to possible sympathisers along their route. They lived in the full presence of the Lord and were open to the movement of the spirit to go wherever was necessary.

The health and growth of the Quaker movement depended on these travelling ministers who published their message and animated groups by their leadership. Before 1652, about 500 people had become sympathetic to Fox's ideas. By 1654 some 5,000 had been convinced and by 1657, the number had exploded to 20,000. Quakers were even undertaking world-wide adventures – to Barbados, Jamaica, North America, the Mediterranean countries, Europe.... If this pace had been maintained, the world would have turned Quaker within a generation!

Divine gift

There have always been Quaker ministers. Friends were no different from other religious groups in believing that the ability to answer to the spiritual needs of others was a gift of the Holy Spirit, rather than a purely human sensitivity. At first the word 'minister' had a loose connotation – it was only later in the 17th century that it gained in precision – and a general distinction can be drawn between Friends who travelled in the ministry and those who stayed at home to care for their local meetings. Those of paramount influence and leadership were generally those who were recognised as having gifts of prophetic insight and powers of persuasive speech, were of clean, sober character and revealed a special quality in their lives.

Within the general body of ministers in Britain was also a group known as Public Friends, whose specific vocation was to travel amongst Friends' meetings to strengthen and encourage them, especially in the London area. It became the custom for all Public Friends who were in London to gather at Gerrard Roberts' house on a Sunday morning so that their activities could be co-ordinated and thus ensure that the available ministerial assistance was spread properly through the city and its surrounding meetings. From 1673, all ministering men Friends who happened to be in London were expected to attend the Second Day Morning Meeting which Fox had set up in order to supervise the distribution of ministry and books. Ministers from all parts had the right of entry and played a full part in the business. Although women ministers were accepted as equal partners, they were not always fully integrated into the administrative structure of the movement.

At first, Morning Meeting met every Monday, although after 1797 it became once a month. It exerted "a tender Christian care" over ministers from overseas who visited London and its vicinity and also considered the religious concerns of ministers liberated by their monthly or quarterly meeting to travel in the service of the gospel abroad, when it was inconvenient to wait for the endorsement of the yearly meeting. Even until 1860, Morning Meeting read and examined all the manuscripts on religious subjects intended for publication by the Society. On the Monday preceding a yearly meeting, this gathering frequently issued epistles and planned ways for increasing the spiritual life and power of the movement.

The custom had prevailed from the beginning of the Morning Meeting for all Public Friends who attended to write their names in its book of ministers. If the name was unchallenged this was considered as equal to recognition or acknowledgement. In 1722, Friend William Gibson arrived and duly entered his name in the book. It was found to be unacceptable to the meeting and the controversy which followed was only resolved by London Yearly Meeting deciding that none other than the properly constituted monthly, quarterly or yearly meetings could disown a minister. After this decision, taken in 1723, no Friend was entitled to be entered in the book as a minister unless he or she produced a certificate from their monthly or quarterly meeting.

Besides the work of addressing meetings among Friends or others, living with remote Quaker groups, making pastoral visits to families, to prisons or political leaders, travelling ministers often forsook their own employment, loved ones and country to travel to far places with no certainty that on arrival the gift of words would be given. They spoke only when they felt themselves moved and delivered only what they believed was given to them. Ministry was unmeditated and spontaneous. The principles that governed were clear. Ministry was a divine gift, freely given and not a matter for human ordination or learning. They who received this gift were to use it, without hire and not as a trade to get money by.

Voluntary contributions towards the support of travelling ministers or their families were sometimes made and documented accounts show that, for example, in Yorkshire, the quarterly meeting gave substantial monetary help – "in token of Friends' love" – to many of its leading ministers, although nothing like a regular stipend was ever paid. In many cases, travelling ministers covered their own expenses and sustained their families without financial help. Local Friends usually watched over the needs of the family or the children of those in prison. They supported the *mission* of opening lives to the continuing and transforming power of the spirit of God – and through this, changing the world – after corporately feeling a call to share in it. After Margaret Fell's convincement in 1652, her home – Swarthmoor Hall in Cumbria – became a support centre for travelling ministers. She passed on news, money, books, little practical comforts and kept them linked together.

Whilst some wives opposed their husbands preaching plans or demonstrated grim resignation to it, others were real comrades in the service. A few Friends however, used the money question as a weapon against the travelling ministers, whom they regarded as puppets of Fox. For example, William Rogers and his supporters are known to have hurled out insults like "parasites", "prating preachers" and "wolves clothed as sheep". Perhaps these Friends were jealous of their influence, an emotion which affected the temper of the Society.

Change and challenge

The loss of leaders during the period of persecution in the late 17th and early 18th centuries seems to have weakened the persuasive spiritual forces in the movement to an extent that was never recovered. With the death of Fox and the 'first publishers of truth', the consequent absence of their extra-ordinary personalities, gifts of leadership, organising capacity, constant intercourse through extensive travel and epistolary correspondence with groups of Friends in Europe and America, the question arose of whether the Society would become a dull and static sect or disintegrate altogether. Friends saw clearly from the beginning that if they were to have no trained clergy, but were seriously to try the great experiment of a priesthood of believers, they had to educate the entire membership of the Society. It was important that provision be made for those Friends who were gifted and might fit themselves to help raise the intellectual and spiritual level of the body.

A way forward was found and for more than a hundred years, a continuous stream of travelling ministers formulated the

Quaker message. Faithful to what they believed was the moving of the Spirit to public ministry, they were recognised by their monthly meetings and recorded as ministers. Thus 'recommended', this decision was then endorsed by the quarterly and ultimately, the yearly meeting. They maintained unity, propagated the spirit, shaped ideals, awakened the youth, established well defined customs, convinced new people to join and encouraged others to recognise their gift to become ministers. Some, such as John Woolman, continued to put the calls of the ministry above their work and wealth. These makers and builders of the Religious Society of Friends were totally absorbed by spiritual ideals; prophetic ministers feeling themselves to be divinely called.

The emphasis of ministry changed somewhat during the 18th century and the position of elders as spiritual overseers strengthened. Early Friends had been outward looking, pushing towards world mission and convinced that people were open to being changed by the ministry of others. Itinerants in this later period were fundamentally concerned with the task of perfecting a 'peculiar people' (ie. God's very own), nurturing persons faithful to their inner light and ready to form a holy, inward life. This era of Quietist ideals tended to devalue the element of mutual help in religious discovery and instead it became a personal and private affair.

Silence and tradition

Circulating yearly meetings were important during the 18th century, moving from place to place within the area of the quarterly meetings which managed them. Rather than meetings for business, they were large, annual, three-day gatherings, held for the purpose of 'spreading the truth'. Through them, itinerant ministering Friends found an opportunity to reach large crowds and to interpret the Quaker message to the membership and the multitude. The crowds were often too large to be held in the local meeting house and in some areas halls were hired, booths erected, barns utilised or gatherings held in the open air. Sometimes 2 or 3 meetings were carried on simultaneously. Visiting ministers bore the main burden although they shared responsibilities with local Friends. Their journals tell of the heavy strain felt. Gradually these meetings disappeared as ministry grew feeble and irrelevant.

Increasing emphasis was put on the importance of silence in worship, driven by a growing ambivalence to vocal ministry. Ministers began to experience great difficulties with their vocation and became apprehensive lest they speak for themselves rather than God. In the increasing absence of other outward expressions of its spiritual life, many parts of the Society began to go cold and the growth of corporate authority gradually resulted in a dearth of fresh, vital leadership.

Friends in the unprogrammed tradition came to distrust theology, be suspicious of doctrine, neglect the Bible, become irritated with ministry which disturbed the silence, and abandon a teaching ministry. Silence was exalted. Anything resembling preaching or evangelism was avoided and as a result meetings were often considered to be lifeless and ministry uninspiring.

Quaker 'tradition' developed, which was what Friends felt to be the best in what they had inherited. The work of ministers became an attempt to articulate the 'tradition' and to complain that people didn't live up to it. Queries were extended to obtain information about the spiritual condition of the Society, thus becoming instruments of control, for they implied what the acceptable answers were.

Social group influence was in powerful operation in 17th and 18th century England. The most effective method employed for construction of the Society was family visiting. Ministers would go from family to family, getting to know all the members and bringing the silent force of personality and influence of ideals. These family 'opportunities' led them to a self searching examination of life and a call to face up to their duties as instruments of the Lord. Ministers would also present the gospel – truth – to those outside the Society, aiming to pick out and win over persons who were disposed towards mystical religion and ready for the type of Christianity which stressed a direct relationship with God and individual responsibility. Gradually, the importance of individual initiative, thrift, avoidance of luxury and debt replaced the united vocation of early Friends to transform the world. Respectability had replaced risk.

However, Friends in this period did produce a form of Quakerism which has endured. Within it grew up several generations which have greatly benefited humanity – inventors, manufacturers, bankers, scientists, social reformers and philanthropists.

Revival

Evangelicalism – characterised by a literal interpretation of the scriptures and widespread missionary effort – entered the Society of Friends in the late 18th century and peaked in London Yearly Meeting in the 1870's. Today the majority of Quakers around the world belong to the pastoral and evangelical tradition. By 1820, London Yearly Meeting had entertained 4 of the most powerful American evangelical ministers – Rebecca Jones, David Sands, William Savery and Stephen Grellet. Between 1810-1840, Morning Meeting, which controlled travelling ministers, allowed William Forster, Anna Braithwaite, Thomas Shillitoe and John Joseph Gurney – all strong evangelicals – to visit America. They preached, promoted Bible societies and encouraged religious education.

In the USA during this period, there were new Quakers on a religious high who needed to be spiritually nourished. Questions arose as to how they were to be shown the importance of the Society's distinguishing testimonies; the relevance of silent worship when entry had been through a revival meeting and full blown preaching of the gospel; and how authoritative answers

14

were to be given to the myriad of questions on doctrine and bible teaching. At first, specially appointed yearly meeting committees experimented with combined monthly meeting support or arranged for unpaid resident ministers to undertake responsibility. This was an adaptation of the institution of the travelling ministry and elders and recorded ministers took part. There were difficulties involving the increasing size of meetings, wide areas over which membership spread, lack of available Friends for ministry and oversight, inabilities to contribute to the costs involved and Friends being too pressed by economic or other circumstances to give time to the discipline of study and meditation. Eventually, a solution was found in which some members were released for full-time pastoral work. This development occurred around the 1880's and was appropriate for the scattered and small meetings. The pastor was considered to be a 'released' Friend, acting as an enabler and helping to develop the gifts of others.

Aware of the American developments, John Wilhelm Rowntree asked at the Manchester Conference in 1896 if it was possible for the Society of Friends to continue as a body of lay people, with all having some responsibility for ministry. Rather than adopt the pastoral system, he proposed the creation of a "Quaker settlement" which would have the form of a permanent summer school – a 'wayside inn' where Friends might find refreshment and repose. George Cadbury put the same point forward more bluntly when he said that "we have had the theory that every man and woman is to be a priest and yet we have done nothing to train them for that office". He felt so strongly that he gave his unoccupied family home of Woodbrooke over to the Society as a college for adults. In 1903, Woodbrooke opened its doors as a liberal Christian think-tank, with opportunities for preparation for vital and efficient vocal and social ministries.

In 1924, London Yearly Meeting decided to end the practice of recording ministers. It was felt that it tended to discourage ministry from many who might feel moved to offer it and gave undue prominence to a restricted number of Friends who appeared to have some kind of 'official' approval. The abolition was not taken lightly. Responsibility to encourage ministry was placed firmly in the hands of monthly meetings.

20th Century

Throughout the 20th century, the travelling ministry has continued with individuals responding to concerns and being supported – or not – by their meetings. However, for a variety of reasons, many Friends have been reluctant to encourage it. As a result of this apparent decline, a concern arose to promote its revival and in 1955, at the conference of the Friends World Committee for Consultation (FWCC) held in Germantown, Ohio, a committee of Friends from five countries was asked to prepare a pamphlet on "Visitation among Friends". Written by Ferner Nuhn, this provided help for a generation of Friends. After the 1979 FWCC Triennial in Gwatt, Switzerland, another committee was formed with the brief to promote travelling under religious concern as an ongoing responsibility of the FWCC. This committee was laid down in 1986.

Another attempt to keep the travelling ministry before Friends was the creation and work of the Home Service Visitation and Extension Committee, with the aim of providing spiritual nurture for the Society in Britain. Although the group itself made several visits to monthly meetings, it appears that little was done to attract real interest. Other examples include the gathering of a group in 1985 to consider the experiences of Barry & Jill Wilshire, travelling with the Quaker Peace Action Caravan and Gillian Hopkins, travelling under concern from Quaker Social Responsibility & Education.

A new development in the travelling ministry occurred in 1990 with the introduction of Joseph Rowntree Quaker Fellowships. This meant that one or two Friends each year, who felt they had a particular contribution to make to the life and thought of the Society of Friends in Britain, could be released

16

from employment for up to one year. During that time, they would travel to meet Friends and others in local meetings, conferences or less formal gatherings. To date, over 10 fellowships have been granted and have included subjects such as community development; cross cultural communication; affirming life's spiritual dimensions; holding tradition, scripture and experience together as a unified whole; ecumenical tensions and the ethics of genetic engineering. Some of these travels are explored later, in part three, the section relating to activity in the 1990's.

Woodbrooke College hosted the 'Equipping for Ministry' conference in 1990, the aim of which was to help the Society look at its present definitions of ministry. Gaps in ministry patterns were highlighted and a challenge thrown out to London Yearly Meeting (LYM) in this minute, which reads in part:

"LYM must recognise the reality of spiritual poverty amongst its members. As one response to this we therefore request this conference to make a public statement saying that there are LYM Friends travelling in the ministry. We ask LYM to consider their support, nurture and funding. There are also other Friends who are called to travel in the ministry. We ask LYM to consider........that existing channels for testing concerns are not always appropriate. Therefore we request that this issue be given space on the YM Agenda as a matter of some urgency."

In 1993, a two-day conference for those travelling in the ministry in Britain was sponsored by Quaker Home Service at Charney Manor (a Quaker retreat and conference centre near Oxford). It was an opportunity for thirty or so contemporary 'travellers' to meet and exchange experiences. Reactions from participants vary from it being positive and helpful to hear first hand experiences, to the disappointment of finding few admitting to travelling in the service of the gospel. Many travelling ministers contacted during my research had only heard of the event after it had taken place. However, according to David Gray, one of the organisers, it revealed a) how many were travelling in the ministry in such a variety of concerns and methods and b) the need for strong support groups from the liberating monthly meeting.

During the 1970's, 80's and 90's, 'official' travelling teams have filled some gaps and met various meetings' needs for education on Quaker issues. Some examples are Quaker Peace Action Caravan, Woodbrooke on the Road, Appleseed, Questabout, Leap and Travelling Light.

To come right up to date, Woodbrooke is launching a new course. Planned to start in October 1997, and open to Friends from all parts of the world, *Equipping for Ministry* is designed as two year open learning covering themes of 'the evolving tradition', 'experience of the Spirit' and 'engagement with the world'. Nurturing one's own ministry – travelling or otherwise – and living as a Quaker in the world today, promise to be major parts.

Life and word

In the silent, unprogrammed tradition, we have become confused about 'travelling in the ministry'. Originally, it referred to labours in the gospel – preaching and sharing the experience of Christ's risen power. Now, many Friends recoil in horror at the thought of proclaiming the 'good news' in such bold terms.

The refrain to 'let our lives speak' glides easily from our lips, but is this enough? Faced with an enquirer and limited time to tell of the Quaker message, we must surely be able to make spoken witness to the personal and group experience of God's presence in our lives, the certainty that the nature of God is love, the confidence that each person can have direct experience of God and that we have a world view that is optimistic and hopeful. Our words may not be perfect but we can be equal to the task of liberating others by the authenticity of our experience, if we are willing to be vulnerable and give something of ourselves away.

18

If we can still lay claim to be a 'priesthood of all believers', we need to come out of our individual and collective shells and show what we have.

The following pages attempt to indicate, in more detail, how this is being done and the way in which we can equip ourselves for more. First, however, it may be useful to see how a 'concern' is recognised, tested and acted upon.

> The Truth is one and the same always, and though ages and generations pass away, and one generation goes and another comes, yet the word and power and spirit of the living God endures for ever, and is the same and never changes.
>
> *Margaret Fell*

2 CONCERN

For early Friends, the most characteristic part of the Quaker life was the serenity, trust and sense of the daily direction which came from the Spirit. The inner light, showing the truth about themselves and the world, led them into a deep unity of love with other humans.

'Ministry', a sharing of insights, given in the light, enabled an understanding of the life and power of truth in each other. A clearly felt call to speak at the meeting to which a Friend belonged was usually accompanied by an emotional tension, trembling and an inner conflict about whether to rise or not. Sometimes, a leading would come to speak elsewhere, or to a non-Quaker group. They would know where to go and what to say. Having obeyed this call, they would then experience inner peace.

This plan of action or 'concern' as it came to be called, was always inwardly initiated and developed. Some of these impulses seemed to border on insanity and it was feared from the beginning that 'messages' might come from other than the Divine Spirit. Therefore, testing the purity of the leading was regarded to be very important. Fox's advice was to first sit with the leadings in patience, in the power and light of God, compare them with similar examples in the Bible and then test them amongst others in the meeting. This process acted as a discipline and led to some Friends being rebuked for ministries which reflected self-ego rather than selflessness.

Elders were responsible for encouraging and nurturing ministry, especially amongst the younger members. Ministers were usually advised to travel in pairs in order to balance individual skills, check each other's leadings and be of mutual support. Many deep rooted partnerships, such as that shown between Edward Burrough and Francis Howgill, remained even when it was necessary to separate temporarily. As with all things experiential, they learned on the job and were often over-eager, even foolish, in the ways they caught public attention. Throughout, however, they remained remarkably clear in the desire to declare their unfamiliar message and to live absolutely for the cause. They faced any sacrifice involved in carrying it out, without compromise.

Testing

Experiences relating to the process of being faithful to a concern are recorded in the journals kept by travelling ministers. Five common and distinct steps can be identified. The time scale for each varies according to the person and can develop over a number of years or be vital and immediate. They are described here using the present tense as they relate to how a concern is recognised and acted upon today – amplification of which can be found in Britain Yearly Meeting's *Quaker Faith and Practice*, paragraphs 13.02-13.18.

Step One or 'Seed phase' – The beckoning or mysterious touch of God upon the soul. This initial, inspirational stage is accompanied by inner conflict and turmoil as the receiver tries to deny it. A period of waiting and prayer is necessary to eliminate the ego, yield to the call and identify the clear message. The call can come at unexpected moments and when the mind is under no kind of religious concern, with the result that one is arrested by something which reaches to the depth of the soul.

Step Two or 'Seedling phase' – Testing the concern by threshing it out, sharing and nurturing it with others in the meeting.

Step Three or 'Fruit formation phase' – Recognition of the concern by the 'home' group. This step involves tenderness and plain speaking of the truth in love if unity with the concern is not felt. The over-riding guiding principle is that it is a leading of the spirit which becomes impossible to resist and not just a strong desire. Consideration is given to the merits and methods of the concern, together with the motivation, character, family and financial situation of the person. If approval and blessing is given, an appropriate minute is written and endorsed by the meeting. This is in effect a letter of recommendation, outlining the nature of the concern, and addressed to all Friends and meetings to be encountered. This minute is usually returned to the meeting on completion of the period of travel, by which time it may have collected endorsements from those who have been visited.

Step Four or 'Ripening phase' – Novitiate period, full of trial and tension, further doubts and inner questioning, struggle and preparation. This period of waiting for clearness indicates whether the time is indeed right for the concern to be acted upon.

Step Five or 'Mature phase' – Surrender and acceptance that one has to go forward with the concern. Inward pressure is usually so clear and confirming that all doubts and hesitations are erased. The call to return, like the call to go, will mysteriously only be heard when the work is accomplished.

Minutes

A *minute of liberation* is one that releases a Friend, under concern, for a particular service. In Britain, this will normally be written by Meeting for Sufferings.

A *travelling minute* is provided by a monthly or yearly meeting for a particular recognised and tested concern. If a visit to another yearly meeting is envisaged, the minute should be forwarded to the home yearly meeting for endorsement – being first clear that the travelling Friend is aware of, and sensitive to, the differences in theology and practice amongst those to be visited. Friends World Committee for Consultation can provide valuable help and guidance for this extended travel.

A *letter of greeting* is one of introduction, issued by a meeting to those of its members or long-term attenders who are travelling – on holiday, in connection with work or for reasons not immediately connected with the service of the Society – and expect to attend meetings for worship in the area visited. It is not a minute of authorisation for any particular service. Return greetings may be written on the letter which is then presented to the issuing meeting on return.

Focusing

Focusing on a particular issue enables those concerned to become 'clear' about possible options and developments which might not have been initially thought about. A 'threshing meeting', to separate 'chaff' from 'grains of truth', can be a useful initial stage for articulating the concern in words that can be understood by a larger number of people. Another method is to hold a 'meeting for clearness', consisting of 4 or 5 trusted Friends, or as many as are interested. They can be arranged privately or by a preparative or monthly meeting, in which case elders and overseers will be consulted. The only qualifications necessary are that those invited are likely to be able to contribute constructively in the process of discernment, be good listeners and maintain confidentiality.

Responsibility

The whole process of recognising and testing the concern carries serious responsibilities for the meeting as well as the individual. Firstly, the meeting should be absolutely clear that it is recognising a religiously valid concern and be willing to be involved in it. Secondly, whether it will give financial or other support for its furtherance. These are vital considerations and must be discussed openly and frankly. Decisions have to be made on the type of support needed, according to individual circumstances and how this will be met. Practical support, in terms of transport, childcare, telephone-link, hospitality and so on could ease the task. Experience has shown that a small group of trusted Friends can be of great help in providing continuous support during the furtherance of the concern, as well as in discerning when the time has come to lay it down. Such a group can be invaluable during 'crises' of one sort or another which will inevitably occur during the travelling period, or for 're-testing' when the waters become muddied. A 'celebration of completion' may be felt to be appropriate and is something that the whole group can be involved in.

Unhurried consideration is very important and it is not unusual for the process to extend over more than one preparative and monthly meeting. If a meeting feels unable to unite with the concern it may suggest a 'holding over' period. Clarity on this is essential for both parties. A meeting may decide to forward the concern to a more widely representative body and again, plain speaking and clear sight is helpful to all concerned. Too often we are afraid of hurting someone's feelings and this tendency leads to the avoidance, rather than acceptance, of responsibility. Sometimes, after a lengthy period of consideration, a meeting may fail to unite with the concern although the person in question might still feel called to continue with it. In such cases, the meeting may encourage the Friend to go forward, although without the support of a minute.

Sending is one thing, the receiving of a travelling Friend, another. They can come from the nearest monthly meeting or the furthest yearly meeting, distance being unlimited in terms of the travelling ministry. The words they use might be difficult to some ears. Personal and group discipline is important in being able to prepare to listen to others and to understand them. How many times have we switched off at the title of the talk or the first uncomfortable word we hear, prejudiced and trapped by our own intolerance? If an invitation comes from a group of worshipping Friends rather than from one or two individuals, responsibility for the person's visit is expected from the whole body. By sharing the tasks of food preparation, accommodation, opening the meeting house, advertising the talk, transport facilitation and so on, everyone can feel involved and committed to the visit. How often in meetings do these things fall to the faithful one or two? In addition, time spent in assessment can be helpful in ensuring that further visits from others can be profitable and easily received. A list of guidelines on responsibilities involved for the traveller and meetings can be found in Appendix A.

.....Do we really know those testimonies and traditions which have grown from the holy experience of many generations of Friends who have lived in close obedience to God's guidance?.....

From the concluding Minute of Central and Southern Africa Yearly Meeting, January 1996

3 TRAVELLING IN THE 1990'S

Throughout this study, I have been amazed at the gifts and skills which are being put to use and it is clear that contemporary itinerant Quakers have a tremendous variety of ministry to offer. In this section, I have tried to give a glimpse of the tempting menus displayed, in the hope that meetings will want to try some for themselves and discover new delights.

Released for a particular service

As Susanne Kromberg's journey amongst Friends in Norway Yearly Meeting was the original inspiration for this book, I will begin here. It also serves to correct some of the balance, as so far much weight has been given to the work of travellers in London – now Britain – Yearly Meeting.

Friends in Norway number around 130. Some 40 of those are geographically isolated and thus virtually cut off from a Quaker spiritual 'blood supply'. Additional factors, especially relating to the increasing age of members, have inevitably led to concerns about how the movement will continue.

At their 1995 yearly meeting, Norwegian Friends made the decision to send Susanne Kromberg out on a fact-finding project, with a travelling minute. The idea for this first came up during Susanne's initial year at the Earlham School of Religion in the USA. Thinking of what to do for the required Field Education, she asked Friends to consider a project of visitation in Norway. At the time, it was regarded more as a research project than travelling in the ministry. The idea was to find out what the needs of the membership were. Funding to carry out this work for one year was thus approved.

One of the first things Susanne did was to write to all the members and regular attenders. The letter contained an introduction of herself, her vision of the Society of Friends, plus

27

nine suggestions of what the project might involve. Friends were asked to help in prioritising but as only a few responded to this specific request, she eventually used the actual visits to do this. In the letter, Susanne said that she would like to visit everyone, with the desire of getting to know each Friend, to learn from/about their spiritual journey and to share her own experiences with them.

Timing of the visits was planned with monthly meeting clerks in order that seminars could be organised or she could attend the monthly meeting sessions. In each region, the clerk was also asked to arrange a social get-together in someone's home. When dates had been fixed, Susanne then wrote to every Friend in the area, inviting them to the particular event, adding that she could make a personal visit if they wished. She then followed up her letter with a telephone call.

Being on a fact-finding mission, Susanne had to speak for the yearly meeting. Because of this, Friends did not necessarily expect or want to talk about spiritual matters. However, in many cases, conversation naturally led to time for reflection, prayer and worship.

A number of Friends were familiar – and comfortable – with 'travelling in the ministry', and used her visit as an opportunity to talk in depth about spirituality. The amount of time spent on each visit varied, often depending on the availability of transport.

Aspects and activities of the project related to five areas of concern:

1) Pastoral care and visiting isolated Friends.
2) Evaluation of Quaker processes in committees and groups.
3) Networking – stimulating active involvement of Friends in their meetings.
4) Seminars on Quaker history, theology and Quaker practices.
5) Publishing a newsletter.

Two fundamental questions were asked:

- ★ What would you want the Religious Society of Friends to be?
- ★ What needs should the Religious Society of Friends meet?

Four basic needs and feelings were identified from the answers:

a) *A need to strengthen the community of Friends and the social bonds between Friends.*

There was a feeling that Friends could not be personal or vulnerable in their worshipping groups because of a lack of trust. Meetings often failed to provide support at the right moment and as a result Friends did not feel able to bring to the meeting what preoccupied them. Ways to improve the sense of community amongst Friends were suggested and included:

- ★ studying Quaker history in order to understand present day diversities;
- ★ guidelines on how to talk about our faith may help us to define what we *do* believe;
- ★ realising that differences between us do not imply superiority;
- ★ discussions of what is meant by tolerance;
- ★ establishing special interest groups within meetings, eg for Christ-centred and liberal Friends, on social concerns or spiritual matters, which can *supplement* joint activities and meetings for worship – thus helping to provide a safer environment in which Friends feel accepted and appreciated;
- ★ more socialising, for those who want or need it;
- ★ exchanges about the small things that enrich our lives rather than abstracts and theories;
- ★ holding religious retreats;
- ★ establishing a group or committee to consider spiritual growth and development and be a contact point for isolated Friends;
- ★ presenting the Society as more 'gathered', naming central issues that *unite* rather than divide.

b) *A need to be more spiritually grounded in the work.*

Too often the Quaker priority is on work. Suggestions to shift the emphasis included:

* learning to be less busy;
* setting priorities and opting for more worship than for committee work and concerns;
* concerns springing from and being guided by meeting for worship;
* avoiding an 'active elite' that monopolises activities, excludes the less active and damages the self-worth of those who feel less able to serve;
* not scaring attenders by expecting them to take on responsibilities too soon.

c) *A dissatisfaction with the way Quaker business methods are applied* led to the realisation of the importance for taking more time and energy to learn about and train ourselves to use the difficult Quaker methods. Specific people may need to be identified to help with this.

d) *A desire to increase membership*

Although this was not seen to be the most important aim, it was recognised that work towards it was necessary. For example:

* developing a good presentation of the Quaker message, remaining loyal to personal experiences and making clear who we are and what binds us together;
* stressing the positive aspects of our 'living faith';
* finding ways into the religious education in schools;
* using the media more actively to present Quaker points of view.

Susanne emphasised that she found a strong desire among Norwegian Friends for spiritual growth and motivation to inspire each other by personal experiences and life stories. She is confident that together, they can make these things happen.

I think it fair to point out that during my research, I could only establish what the project entailed and the results as compiled by Susanne herself. Although I wrote to Norwegian Friends known personally to me, I have not been able to discover what the reaction of the membership has been to the project's findings or what the next steps are likely to be.

Explorations and possibilities

Susanne talked about the project at the FWCC Europe and Middle East Section (EMES) gathering at Easter 1996. Interest groups discussed the content of her talk and made a number of suggestions for the Section's yearly meetings and groups to consider. These were circulated and included:

1. Travelling among Friends in Europe

– Using Susanne's model, pay a person to travel throughout the Section to talk to meetings and isolated Friends about their needs and to gather ideas;
– Holding local interest or discussion groups with well-known Friends, opening such meetings to outsiders and publishing events in the local press;
– Encouraging exchange visits between meetings and for certain periods of time in order to develop friendships and community;
– Making appropriate funding available.

2. Meeting the needs of children and families

– Using existing study packs on the specific needs of children and families in meetings (Quaker Home Service, UK, and Philadelphia YM, USA);
– Taking turns at going out from meeting for worship with the children and/or having regular special meetings which involve them (combined with potluck dinner, interest group on children's needs or child-oriented events);
– Welcoming families and children at any meeting for worship;
– Make 'children' the theme of a regional meeting or conference.

3. Reception and needs of newcomers

– Welcome and talk to them, be sensitive to how far they want to be involved, plan a study programme or worship sharing sessions on topics they are interested in;

– Be open about one's own spiritual needs;

– Be aware of who we Quakers are and how we present ourselves.

4. Keeping up the life of the Meeting

– By trying new things and keeping at it to make them work;

– Maintaining and circulating ideas of things that have/have not worked for other meetings and using also modern communication media;

– Combining meetings with shared meals or outings in order to spend longer time together;

– Opening the meeting once a month to a discussion about real issues facing society in general;

– Hosting and promoting retreats.

Follow up

The Europe and Middle East Section's Executive Committee was asked to consider these suggestions in order that it might be seen how to support new initiatives of travelling in the ministry, visitation and retreats. At the 1997 Section Meeting, further discussion took place. Although no definite conclusions were reached, there was a sense of wanting to encourage and support such activity, although the inclusive term of *visiting* was preferred.

The Section stressed the need for sensitivity and care so that meetings would not feel imposed upon. It was emphasised that visitors should be sure that they are the right person to make a specific visit and that the recognised testing process has been followed. Willingness to make financial resources available for visiting, from the Section's special fund, was expressed. A proposal to establish a co-ordination group is to be taken forward.

Travelling in the listening ministry

We often misunderstand what someone is saying because we have failed to listen. How often have we wished that we could be listened to? True listening is active rather than passive and, needing skill and practice, is a difficult discipline.

The Northern Friends Peace Board's 1993 Annual Report, states that there are many parts of Britain in which meetings are small and where individual Friends are scattered and geographically isolated from one another. Amidst such isolation, there is a tendency for Friends not to travel to conferences or think themselves to be large enough in number to consider hosting workshops. With the aim of meeting with some of these isolated Quakers in its catchment area, the Board appointed two pairs of Friends to travel to parts of the North and West of Scotland in 1993. From the outset, and in preparatory discussions with Friends in these areas, the emphasis was on travelling with a *listening* ministry.

Founded in 1913, with the mandate '*to advise and encourage Friends in the north (of Britain), and through them their fellow Christians and citizens generally, in the active promotion of peace in all its height and breadth*', the Board hoped that through such an activity it could become more aware of the needs of Friends and therefore be in a better position to provide the support and nurture recognised as being part of its responsibility.

In 1994, following the success of the visits to Scotland, two Friends were invited to visit meetings on the Isle of Man. Again, a number of issues were raised and considered. It was found that the listening ear – and heart – of an outsider can be a helpful means of addressing some of the range of peace-related issues which meetings find difficult to tackle on their own. According to the Board's 1995 Annual Report, two Friends visited Shetland in that year and the working group, set up to monitor the project of the listening ministry, began an assessment of the work.

Visits were initially arranged through direct contact with the Board's full-time co-ordinator, and in consultation with a local Friend. For later visits, only the initial contact and arrangement of dates was the responsibility of the co-ordinator, with itinerary planning being left to the travelling Friends appointed by the Board. In general, the wider the geographical area which has needed to be covered, the longer the visit has been. The physical act of travelling itself requires stamina and when combined with meetings with Friends it has been essential to have some space built into the time-table in order to recover energy and prepare for intensive discussions.

The structure of the visits has varied – from one-to-one conversations in private homes, conversations in cars en route from one place to another, periods of worship or workshop-style activities. The travellers have used the visits as opportunities to tell Friends something about the current work and concerns of the Board, trying as much as possible to use that as a starter for discussion and exchange of ideas, visions, hopes, fears and difficulties connected with the concept of peace.

The experience has clearly shown that an outsider visiting a group adds a new dimension to the discussion or conversation that takes place. It was also discovered that, throughout the presence and gentle questioning of the travellers, some Friends seem to have heard one another in new ways. On other occasions, they have helped to open up areas of discussion or an awareness of a concern that continues in that meeting after the visit. Whilst the travellers were not appointed to act specifically as counsellors or mediators, it has sometimes been right to do what they could in those areas.

Practical points to emerge have included the importance of beginning the travel with a small meeting for worship; having a partnership of an older and younger Friend which enables a wider sharing of skills and experience; the necessity for both to be trained in the areas of listening and facilitation and to have organisational ability; the need to maintain transparency and confidentiality; and finally, the value of the Board's oversight group, set up for the purpose of support, clarification of aims and methods and final evaluation in confidence.

For the future, the Board envisages the possibility of sending Friends in the listening ministry to *all* meetings in their area, upon invitation. There is much to be gained in understanding how Friends can best be helped to live the peace testimony.

The Joseph Rowntree Quaker Fellowships

The purpose of the Fellowships is to enable one or two Friends who feel that they have a particular contribution to make to the life and thought of the Society of Friends in Britain to spend about a year free of the need to earn their living. During that time, it is expected that they will travel to meet Friends, be thought-provoking and even challenging, in order to develop insights into the world in which they live and share experiences which would strengthen the spiritual life of the Society. Possibilities for less conventional ways of getting together with Friends and for involving other religious groups are envisaged and encouraged.

The 'home' meeting is asked to indicate its views about the application, although it is recognised that some may be from those whose relationship with their meeting is not always comfortable. Hence a successful application does not depend on the support of the meeting but it is important for the Trustees to be aware of the meeting's attitude. A support group is seen as being vital to the would-be Fellow, in order to provide eldership and oversight during the period. Members of such a group should have appropriate insights and skills and enough time to provide support and feed-back.

A Fellowship will normally compensate for loss of earnings and, where an applicant is currently unwaged, a personal allowance is calculated on the basis of previous earnings or some other reasonable sum.

Many Joseph Rowntree Fellows have continued their work in various ways after the 'official' year was completed. For example, one now runs a small Retreat Centre, another is working on 'The Connections Project' to assist the growth of adult religious learning and spiritual nurture in Britain Yearly Meeting and a third is continuing to offer workshops, worship sharing and radical bible study.

In order to get first hand knowledge about the success of completed Fellowships, I contacted Friends who had been appointed by the scheme. Studying their answers and comments has been a fascinating exercise. In order to respect confidentiality, I have reported the findings as factual, without crediting anything in particular to anyone.

The Concerns have included the threats and promises of ecumenical issues; cross-cultural communication; community development in Quaker meetings; affirming life's spiritual dimensions; and holding tradition, scripture and experience as a unified whole.

Reaching ..... those who were concerned/happy about decisions taken by Britain Yearly Meeting in joining the Council of Churches for Britain and Ireland; those interested in inter-faith relationships; Friends, Attenders and wider faith communities; those longing for a deeper approach to prayer and a sense of Presence; those searching for a specifically Quaker understanding of Christian truth.

Presentations included ..... producing leaflets which outlined various ways of working and the subjects on offer; workshops, retreats, conferences, talks, reflections, weekend gatherings; case studies of selected meetings; articles in journals; art and meditation sessions; Ignatian guided prayer; Jungian/ experiential bible days; using specific themes such as creation, peace, community etc.

Difficult times came when ..... the inviting meeting had not fully prepared for the visit; prejudices, racism and the intolerance of Friends came to the surface, leading to anger and frustration for both parties; the traveller had too high an expectation; there were anxieties about an expenses budget thus skimping on taxi fares, leading to lonely experiences on dark nights in strange cities; there was a large geographical distance from the 'home' support group; the nature and demands of the project undertaken seemed to be overwhelming; Friends appeared jealous and resentful of the 'official' nature of the fellowship.

Overcoming these difficulties by ..... sharing the experiences with the support group; expressing the anger to selected people; meditating and praying about the issues; continuing with the work knowing that the call to do it was still there; giving oneself treats; realising that the feelings would pass; talking to trusted individuals; re-assessing the material used and trying a different/more attractive type of presentation.

Needs of Friends visited included ..... having sufficient time and information to make important decisions which are likely to affect the whole Society; being able to express themselves and their beliefs without fear of ridicule or criticism; being able to express emotions; being able to talk about personal problems – marriage difficulties, homosexual orientation, children and their needs; being able to talk to a 'neutral' person who would be coming and going away again; being 'heard'; the desperate need for teaching (about the scriptures, testimonies, Quaker business methods etc); a longing to hear the word of God; re-discovering the Quaker identity.

Using the term 'travelling in the ministry'? ....Two did not use it as they felt themselves to be carrying out a research project on behalf of the Joseph Rowntree Charitable Trust; one used it but felt that, in general, Friends were uncomfortable with it; another used it happily because it was felt to be appropriate to the 'gospel' theme, in its broadest sense; another didn't make use of it for the purpose of the fellowship year, but did so afterwards.

The future of 'travelling in the ministry' was envisaged like this ..... the need for thorough testing of the concern and adequate funding of the work to be taken forward; helping to make the concept better known and *understood* amongst Friends; further considerations of how travelling ministers are financially and pastorally supported; the avoidance of creating a new elite of 'hired priests'; encouraging more travelling/intervisitation at the local level; paying attention to 'post-travelling' time and supporting (in various ways) those whose experience leads them to continue to work on the themes of concern; the necessity of identifying those with a calling, giving basic teaching and mentoring plus ongoing support (counselling, listening); the recognition of 'spontaneity' (set off and go at one's own cost); the need for accountability – to the Society in general as well as the 'sending' body; and having a radical vision ....

Ministry in the gospel of Jesus Christ

Preaching and sharing the experience of Christ's risen power was the original meaning of travelling in the ministry. I have heard Friends, in various countries, express a sense of complete isolation from those they worship with because they are prevented from talking about their faith experience in plain, Christian terms. For them, such language is natural and conveys truth and reality as they perceive it. So often however, the very words 'minister', 'gospel', 'Jesus' and 'Christ' bring up all sorts of negative reactions in others and inevitably barriers are erected.

There are travelling ministers today who are driven by the call to share the Christian message with everyone, within or outside the Society of Friends. Their concern is to recover the message that early Friends preached so powerfully – that *'Christ has come to teach his people himself'*. During their travels, they have witnessed individuals who long to hear the word of God.

In those same meetings, there are also Friends who will stop at nothing to quench that word. As a result, some have moved on to other churches because they haven't received the kind of teaching and nurture they longed for. Many worship with other Christians in order to fill the gaps in their spiritual lives. We say that it is alright for people to move on. But is this opting out of facing the responsibility of doing something to provide the spiritual bread that is needed? Are we turning our friends away empty handed and if so, why?

In contrast to the early Quakers, today's Friends of the silent, unprogrammed tradition are a generation who have little acquaintance with the scriptures. Those who travel in the gospel ministry try to make that literature worthy of investigation, but the task is monumental. For some, the affirmation that 'Christ has come to teach his people himself' has no relevance, while for others this is still the backbone of their Quaker understanding.

Those who feel particularly called to express their Christ-based experience within this tradition are active, yet few. Members of the New Foundation Fellowship (UK), individuals like Charles G. Lamb (Ireland Yearly Meeting) and Teresa Hobday (Britain Yearly Meeting) struggle to be heard. By taking the time to hear what they say, we can find ourselves coming closer to an understanding of what their real message is.

Teresa Hobday, Charles G. Lamb and Ursula Windsor have written much of their thoughts and experiences and for this section I have drawn on their papers and letters in my attempt to analyse their different gospel ministries. Putting them together in this section however does not imply that they use the same words, or a similar approach.

The Concern

A concern about the spiritual apathy found amongst Friends, who so often speak in intellectual terms, very eloquently and with sound reasoning, is the motivation for travelling in this ministry. It is felt that the initial great revelation of God to George Fox, that there is one who can speak to our condition and in whom all things are made new – namely, Christ Jesus – is missed. In order to be faithful to their concern, Friends have sought the support of their meetings and as a result have been given a travelling minute.

Ministry

Vocal ministry is often the primary means of communication and in the course of the travel visits have been made to private homes, hospitals and places of work. It has also meant being practical, picking up a spade or paintbrush so that one can get close beside another and demonstrate – as well as talk about – one's faith. Often, travelling ministers have been brought into confidences never before related and have given comfort by the very act of listening. By gently sharing one's own experience of how difficulties have been overcome by a personal faith in Christ and his teachings, things can begin to make sense to another.

It is necessary to be sensitive to unspoken needs and questions. Listening can sometimes mean being prepared to come away from a meeting without having had a chance to speak or talk on the planned subject. Realising that one may succeed where least expected is the other side of the coin. The ministry of letter writing that can follow, with opportunities for deepening understanding and relationships, has also proved to be an important part of the work.

Difficulties

Difficult situations have included finding oneself newly arrived in a country, full of confidence. Within hours, all has gone. A thief has knocked you down and run away with everything you possess. Alone and afraid, standing only in shirt, trousers and shoes, one is forcefully reminded of the temptations to exert the self-ego. In such situations one learns at first-hand how to rely on God. From that particular brutal experience came an ability to minister fully to the needs of others later encountered at a gathering of Friends.

Other hard lessons learned have included being forced to recognise one's own ego-centred ministry; realising the dangers of submitting to compromise rather than being true to a strongly felt leading; having to ditch already made elaborate plans; and humbly recognising that God was the 'leader of the expedition'.

Expenses

These are often met out of one's own pocket. On occasions, travel expenses have been paid for by the inviting group. Quaker Trusts have also made grants. Sometimes, meetings and churches have insisted on giving money for conducting services but such money has been received only on the understanding that the donor realised that it was going to be handed on to the organisation who had paid for the travel. On other occasions, monies have been returned to the giver, *"stating as it does in the scriptures, freely you have received, freely give"*. A characteristic of this ministry is the faith that if the call is true, ways will open to make it possible.

Intervisitation

Quaker Faith & Practice 13.29: (1925,1994)

We urge Friends, when staying away from home during holiday or on business, to attend a meeting for worship if there is one within reach. Such attendance may well have the effect of strengthening the meeting, and of helping Friends who were hitherto strangers to know one another.

When visiting meetings in another yearly meeting be careful not to be a burden.

Personal experience

When Franco Perna and I visited Quaker meetings in Australia, Aotearoa/New Zealand and Singapore during the turn of the

41

year 1994/5, we took with us a letter of greeting from the FWCC International Membership Committee, then acting as our 'overseers'. As isolated Friends, living in Italy and therefore unattached to a monthly or yearly meeting, we didn't have regular access to a 'home' group of Quakers.

Our reception in those countries was warm and loving and we were given ample opportunity to talk of our experiences of grass-roots peace initiatives in former Yugoslavia, where we had worked as volunteers. In turn, we learned about issues they were involved in. Friends sent their greetings to FWCC by writing their pieces on 'our letter' and more than once expressed appreciation for this chance to feel part of the worldwide Quaker family. Once back home, we returned it to the FWCC World Office, thus completing the circle.

It isn't possible for us to obtain such a letter every time we travel somewhere – often at the drop of a hat – so we visit meetings without this 'official' introduction. Nevertheless, on the continent of Europe and indeed in Latin America, we have been given an opportunity to tell something of our activities and interests. Furthermore, by accompanying Cuban pastors on their home visits to Friends in outlying villages – often walking long distances on rough roads due to lack of available transport, we have become acutely aware of their deep faith and commitment and learned much from them.

We have never thought of, or promoted ourselves, as 'travelling in the ministry', but this is how some Friends have comfortably described us. Indeed it was a shock and an embarrassment to us when, out of the blue, we were given some financial support by one particular meeting in Australia.

Our main role is one of communication, dialogue and networking – informing about various Quaker events that we have participated in, travels and contacts we have made, and discovering what the meeting and its members are involved in.

Some of our time is spent in Britain and there, sadly, our experience has been less positive. Usually, after meeting for worship, clerks welcome visitors in one all-encompassing sentence without giving a space to pass on greetings from another worshipping body. We have even experienced the 'cold-shoulder' treatment as Friends gather into small groups over coffee, leaving the visitor alone to study the notices and posters pinned up on the wall. There are notable exceptions of course, for which we are grateful.

Negatives are usually balanced by positives. During our extensive three month travel in Latin America, we discovered the whereabouts and time of the nearest Quaker meeting and went along to worship with them. We hadn't asked for a letter of greeting – this time a more complicated affair with Franco in international membership and myself a member of Switzerland Yearly Meeting. Instead, Loida Fernandez – the FWCC worker based in Mexico – with whom we had been in close contact about our visit, wrote to the Quaker churches on our route, introducing us and telling a little of our background and interests.

In addition, during a 2 day stay at Quaker House in Managua, Nicaragua, Friends spontaneously wrote a letter of greeting for us to take to Friends in Mexico and Cuba. In this letter, our names were mentioned and reference made to the rich exchange we had been able to make with them. Friends in both these countries appreciated this loving and thoughtful gesture.

Contact and friendship does not end when the visit is over. Witness to this is the considerable amount of correspondence to be handled once we are back home.

Travelling in friendship

There are others who are involved in visiting far flung meetings. For many it is interconnected with a concern for Friends in a particular area, such as Eastern Europe. Sensitive visits to people who feel themselves to be geographically, politically and economically isolated can be a moving ministry. Friends who have helped by sharing their experiences of such travels include Eva Pinthus, Brian Bridge, Marianne Boelsma and David Pulford. By using responses to my questionnaire, reading their detailed reports and through personal conversations, some of their experiences can be illustrated.

Where do they go?.......Czech Republic, Slovenia, Hungary, Eastern Germany, China, Botswana, Lesotho, South Africa.

Who are they hoping to reach?......Friends, sympathisers, other believers and young people, as well as politicians and civil servants.

What do they do?........ encourage and listen; talk about a different way of doing things, a Quaker witness; facilitate meetings when it seems right; visit those who are thinking of applying for membership; bring experience of retreats and quiet days; impart skills such as spiritual journal writing; join in worship sharing and discussions; bring news from abroad .....and vice versa; *'be'* with people rather than carrying out specific activities (a 'ministry of presence'); take naturally arising opportunities for conversation on spiritual matters; help with young people's programmes and sessions on Quaker understanding.

Who are they accountable to?....their preparative and monthly meetings; Trustees who have given financial support; Quaker committees.

Do they have a 'support base'?.....individuals who know them well and have time for listening and advising; a small group of Friends set up by their local meeting for the purpose of support; private quiet time for reflection; a strong belief in being called, by God, to the service.

Do they use the term 'travelling in the ministry'? One answered with a resounding 'yes', with a qualification that she probably uses it more widely than Fox would have done. Another hesitated, not using it at first but feeling easier about it now that Friends in the local meeting understand it as a 'ministry of exploration'. One more felt the term to be daunting and awesome and hesitated to use it on its own, preferring the explanation of 'travelling under a concern rooted in the Spirit' to describe the activity. He points out that if one defines 'travelling in the ministry' as one being undertaken by a 'recorded minister', who travels in gospel labour accompanied by an elder or other sound Friend, then he is not entitled to use it. However, as he believed his labours to be true to the Spirit, the meaning, rather than the words themselves, mattered most.

How do they see the future of the travelling ministry?..... the importance of reviving the tradition of travelling in pairs; working in partnership with elders; having the physical fitness to continue; enabling Friends to step out of their usual spiritual and social routines and take a quiet time in the busy working week; facilitating opportunities for attenders and enquirers to ask questions which they might not feel comfortable asking members of their own meeting; continuing to provide an impartial listening ear; bringing fresh visions into particular situations; giving people the greatest gift of all – time; the need for younger Friends to be able to travel in the ministry.

Who pays?....travellers themselves, although at times financial support may come from local meetings, Trusts or even through specific fund-raising events.

Groups

Group journeys, such as those organised to visit Quakers in Bolivia, Cuba, the Middle East and Nicaragua, can also be put into this section. The help-links which can result are valuable, such as those fostered by *Quaker Bolivia Link*; the *Cuban Quaker Project* (run jointly by Miami programmed and unprogrammed meetings); and *Quaker Friends of Cuba*. Their addresses (together with other useful ones), can be found in Appendix B.

Travelling and teaching

Woodbrooke on the Road is an excellent example of a teaching service which is mobile, well prepared and readily available to meetings – whether in Britain or abroad, in English and other languages. David Gray, now retired from the Woodbrooke teaching staff, gives insight on the value of the enterprise and its contribution to the life of the Society.

Aims

It began in 1977, when David was appointed as a Woodbrooke staff member with the brief of planning and co-ordinating 'off-campus' teaching. The resulting travelling teaching service was, in effect, a travelling classroom. The aim was to reach 1000 Quakers and Attenders, per year, in their meetings. Between 1977 and 1994, (when David retired), about 250 *On the Road* events were presented, mostly in Britain, but including 27 different countries worldwide. Overseas Yearly Meetings were appreciative, especially when teaching was in their own languages.

The "basic" *On the Road* event comprised 2 tutors (one of them always a current Woodbrooke teaching staff member), 30 members of the Quaker worshipping community, a meeting house, and a weekend. Topics such as "Basic Quakerism", "Quakers today", "Being a member of a meeting", "What do we do during meeting for worship", "The Quaker business method", "Quaker history", "Revising our book of discipline" and "Questions and Counsel", illustrate the variety offered.

Response

The response from meetings was always superb and exhilarating, giving one the energy and enthusiasm to go on with the work. Many meetings invited the team back several times (11 was a record!), using the service to encourage and strengthen the life of the worshipping community.

Occasionally meetings which invited the teams did so because they felt that they were in difficulties and that *On the Road* could provide a sort of 'Flying Doctor' service. While the teams never claimed to be therapeutic or 'trouble shooters', their presence *did* often help meetings which were feeling fragile. They did this by teaching the Quakerism that Friends needed to know and practise better.

David regrets that *Woodbrooke on the Road* was never invited to teach at pastoral and/or evangelical meetings and was thus limited to the unprogrammed, liberal tradition. Neither did other denominations or faiths take up the offer of a visit.

Ministry

As a paid professional, doing the teaching job that he was employed and qualified to do, David didn't use the term 'travelling in the ministry' to describe the service. In his opinion, this description is limited to those voluntarily travelling under a sense of concern that has been tested and authorised by a monthly meeting.

There were times of feeling lonely and isolated whilst travelling on-the-road. David comments that the service was somewhat "invisible" to others at the college and they sometimes forgot that it existed. Out of curiosity, I looked for details of it in the 1997-98 Woodbrooke programme of term-time events and short courses, and could not find any. All I discovered was a small sentence at the end of the section on what was on offer and a box to tick if information about *On the Road* was required.

Variety

From his involvement in setting up the Quaker Home Service conference on 'travelling in the ministry' (1993) and the experience of visiting so many meetings, David has realised the enormous variety of the itinerant ministry and its benefits to the Society. If one includes 'official' or 'semi-official' teams such as Quaker Peace Action Caravan, Leap, Questabout, Travelling

Light and The Leaveners; individual Friends who feel led to travel and minister to meetings without invitation, monthly meeting sanction or support minute; visiting holidaymakers; teams like Appleseed or services like Bumblebee; those who are paid to do it and those who are not; the combination of yearly meeting officers, FWCC staff and committee members; the eleven *On the Road* overseas study tours for Friends to meet and study Quakerism in the Middle East, China, USA and Canada and so on, one comes to a recognition of incredible resources.

> ...As petals form a beautiful flower, so Friends form a word-wide community – differently sharing the same fragrance of love and concern. The lamps may be different but the light is the same, it comes from beyond...
>
> *Epistle from FWCC Asia West Pacific Section Meeting, July 1996*

4 WIDER QUAKER MINISTRIES

In the introduction, reference was made to Edgar G. Dunstan's provocative words, *"Have you anything to declare?"* If Quakers in the 'unprogrammed' tradition have difficulty with a response, there are parts of the world where Friends can answer with a resounding *Yes*. Theirs is a way of 'programmed' worship, with hymns, prayers and preaching, an emphasis on the authority of the Bible and a belief in Christ as their personal saviour.

Within this tradition are a number of different expressions of faith and practice, making it impossible to affix labels to any particular one. Inter-mixtures of 'conservative', 'liberal', 'charismatic', 'pastoral', 'evangelical' and others, abound. Yet, they all feel part of one single world-wide Quaker family.

Joyful growth and outreach

Their numbers are enviable, exceeding those of the silent tradition. Children, young adults, the middle and later years are all fully represented. Multiplication is by evangelisation, to anyone who will listen, sharing the good news of Christ as they have experienced it for themselves.

Often facing hardships due to socio-economic and political conditions, their lives are far from comfortable, although conversations constantly refer to the love, joy and deep meaning found through receiving God into their hearts and following Christ's example. Aware of a world filled with injustice, inequality, racism and thousands of hidden problems, they believe that their purpose on earth is to be like salt and light (Matthew 5:13-14).

Many of them would say that individualism has the effect of turning the Quaker family into an end in itself. By their sense and practice of community, conviction that they are God's instruments in the world is colourfully illustrated.

One finds pastors of both sexes working together to develop their Quaker communities and reaching outwards. Their role is seen to be one of helping others to realise and carry out their own ministries, rather than being the authoritative 'minister'. Quaker colleges facilitate study and practice in this particular ministry and, on successful completion of the course, an individual is entrusted with the development of a Friends church community. The pastor's work includes home visitation, visits to hospitals, facilitating the growth of Bible and Quaker practice study groups, encouraging and developing activities for the youth, counselling, oversight of the evangelisation programme and much more. Their homes are often 'open house' for members of the congregation to come and talk and be listened to.

Friends other than the pastor can be regularly found leading the Quaker meeting, with prayer, song or address. Young pastors 'in-training' are given the opportunity to learn on the job by circulating amongst the churches of the area. 'Shadowing' a more experienced pastor, they can gain confidence, talk things over and be encouraged to develop their own special gifts.

Misunderstandings

In some countries where 'programmed' Friends are to be found, the linkage with Quaker practice, as we might know it, appears to be tenuous. For example, where pastors are male, decision making authoritarian, reference to George Fox scanty and outward social and political witness virtually nil. Indigenous cultures and traditions overlay and interweave to result in practices some find difficult to accept as 'Quaker'. On the other hand, responding to the call to be peacemakers, many have appealed to their governments to exempt young Christians from obligatory military service.

One of the disappointments is the feeling that Friends from other traditions don't take the trouble to understand them. In a limited survey amongst 'unprogrammed' Friends, undertaken in connection with research for this book, the findings were interesting.

There were some 'don't knows'. However, one person was very comfortable with 'translating' European Quaker terms into evangelical ones and vice-versa. She could cheerfully – and without hesitation – admit to being 'saved' because, for her, the meanings mattered more than the words. Another was troubled by the aggressiveness and male dominance often associated with evangelising. Someone was uncomfortable with a Quakerism that omitted the peace testimony, substituted a pastoral system and hierarchy for a 'priesthood of all believers', sidelined women and younger adults and by-passed the Quaker business method. There was also discomfort with a 'personal salvation' approach, and a rating of the Bible as the *word*, rather than words of God. Another Friend gave an affirmation that the gospel of Jesus Christ can cut right to the heart of life and felt that 'sin' and 'satan' needed to be mentioned, otherwise people can easily 'sweep things under the carpet'.

Bridges

Conferences and seminars, such as those organised between countries and on a world-wide basis make contact and conversation possible. Specific inter-continent visitations, such as those envisaged by the FWCC Section of the Americas among and between north-south, south-north and south-south, can help to widen, lengthen and strengthen bridges which are already in place, as can casual ones from travelling Friends from other traditions.

Fostering such encounters leads to realising that we are all seeking that of God in everyone, striving to live honestly, simply and in peace, following the leadings of the Holy Spirit. We don't need to lose our own ways. Rather, being secure in our faith leads to an ability to understand and sympathise with people from a broad range of perspectives, without fear. By focusing on love, we can be united. Concentrating on our differences and words which mean different things to others can drive us apart.

Although not a travelling one as we might understand it, the pastoral ministry has much to offer in terms of outreach and the development of community and we would do well to learn from it. Inhibitions about giving our testimonies and speaking of our own spiritual experiences can vanish in the face of gentle encouragement from those whose joyful songs express complete faith, hope and love for God. The words might be difficult for us, but the meaning of offering one's life for another is real.

So this is a challenge to you. Leave Jerusalem and go and preach to the Gentiles. Because when we have met you – you silent Quakers whose thinking we know so well – I repeat, love has united us...... I believe that this is a challenge that God is putting before us...... a new focus through which we may question everything we are thinking, a new focus through which we may let the Spirit penetrate our lives ....

Heredio Santos (Cuba), 1993

5 WHAT HAPPENS NEXT?

Observations

From personal experience, travellers have found that a 'flying visit' is not a satisfactory way to visit meetings and ideally it was felt important to stay for a weekend and to join in the life of the group. In such a relaxed environment, with time at hand, individuals can take advantage of the offer of a pair of listening ears. The travellers have often found themselves in a catalyst role, enabling Friends to share their doubts and convictions with each other in a way that may not have happened without the input of a third party.

A strong, motivated support group was seen as an essential and integral part of the travelling ministry. In travelling alone, isolation is often experienced, especially in times of difficulty or when tiredness sets in. Knowing there was access to a group or individual was, apart from anything else, a great psychological boost.

The fundamental problem of a lack of Quaker identity has repeatedly been expressed by those 'travelling in the ministry' and it seems essential that, somehow, our meetings need to become corporate communities rather than a set of individuals on their own spiritual quest. Whilst Friends – particularly those of the unprogrammed tradition – are in such a state of confusion, it seems impossible to validate teaching and preaching ministries, in the broadest sense possible.

Travellers have also observed that Friends are overburdened and the last thing they want is to be continually urged to take on more commitments. A shift of emphasis to *'being'* rather than 'doing', has been expressed. In an age of busy timetables, the role of meeting for worship in a teaching ministry might need to be examined.

The ability to communicate the message of the heart needs nurturing so we can be free to express the validity and worth of our own experience. The need for help in discerning one's gifts, validating and using them in the service of others is something which has to be recognised.

A final observation is that the anti-authoritarian culture and tradition of 'unprogrammed' Friends leads to problems in supporting individuals who feel called to the service of 'travelling in the ministry'. The passive and/or aggressive response towards those who exhibit gifts of spiritual leadership can often mean loss of those who feel called to respond to a concern. 'Travelling in the ministry' is something that has to be worked on *together* – if the grass-roots membership want to take it forward.

Pointers

Several people have pointed out that we live under different times and circumstances than those of early Friends. Whilst recognising the validity of that, I think that we have to learn from the great achievements of the past if we want to address the enormous challenges of the present and the future. There is still a need to be 'convinced', to know the divine life and power and open our lives to the same transforming truth known by those who came before us.

Although the Quaker movement has been affected over the centuries by traditions, customs, structures and ideas which have changed the nature of it, fascinating pointers for the future have emerged, which give me a sense that travelling under concern is still a necessary part of our Quaker witness.

The main features for exploration thus appear to centre on our corporate need to:

a) re-discover our Quaker identity; b) find the confidence to express our faith; c) listen and be listened to; d) develop our sense of community; e) learn about and apply our Quaker practices; f) attract and encourage people of all ages to worship with us.

All these are interwoven and one of the most important dynamics is that of trust. We need to feel safe, value and trust each other. This does not just happen. It comes out of worshipping, talking, studying, working, eating, praying and being together.

Deepening the spiritual life

Deepening the spiritual life of the meeting may be something we have given a low priority to. Edward Hoare, in his booklet *Deepening the Spiritual Life of the Meeting*, helpfully points us towards two aspects.

The first is the individual responsibility of each member to try to grow closer to God. The second is the responsibility of the community to work together to help each individual on their spiritual journey. He goes on to say that it is in the community that the individual can test what may seem to be the leadings of the Spirit against the working of the Spirit within the group.

Friends within the unprogrammed tradition have spoken of the lack of nurturing for those who find themselves called to minister. All too often, approaches to elders of a meeting have led to frustration and a feeling of a 'wilderness' within. Increasingly, gatherings of monthly meeting elders are poorly attended and an air of indifference and neglect pervades.

We seem to be shy of trusting our experience of the indwelling divinity. We are afraid about sharing that experience with others. In community we can test our words and what is in our hearts, thus gaining confidence to speak of it with others we encounter in our daily lives. My own experience is such that one doesn't need to 'push' any message. Ordinary conversations naturally seem to lead to the moment of such sharing and equally, if sensitive, one knows when the time is not right.

Finding answers

As has been illustrated in the previous pages, travelling Friends can be helpful in the process of working towards identity, community, learning, testing and communicating. Through their presence, meetings have been able to find their own answers to questions that trouble them. Through a fresh vision and patient listening which allows another to find and explain themselves, confidence in the divine experience can grow and blossom. Helpful teaching, which strengthens the weak spots, is also appropriate.

One of our difficulties lies in the word 'ministry'. If gospel ministry in its broadest sense is about the divine light (of Christ, or however one is comfortable in describing it) illuminating the things in life which we have to change, – then either we have to face up to what the light reveals, or hide from it. Held back by our own interpretations and prejudices, we are prevented from being freed to the full height, depth and breadth of its meaning.

Understanding and involvement in the process of how a concern arises, is tested, acted upon and laid down, are essential. If we are not clear, we get muddled and lose sight of what we are to do. Young people in our midst need guidelines and support if they are to be enabled to take forward their own concerns. Being inspired by others can play a large part in this. David Pulford reports that his 'travelling in friendship' within Central and South Africa Yearly Meeting appears to have inspired a younger member to travel among Young Friends.

Testing a concern can be difficult or impossible for those who are isolated individuals, without access to regular, worshipping communities. Many monthly meetings are so poorly attended that they may no longer be fertile ground for testing – or supporting – a concern. Adjusting the process to fit the reality of the situation is important.

Support is recognised as being necessary, yet another problem lies with our timidness to discuss matters financial. It is unusual for a Friend under concern to be in a position to meet all the related costs. If we fail to address the matter, we relinquish trust in the person, in ourselves, in the process. The question of accountability also arises. To whom, and how, should this be demonstrated?

Spontaneity and a sense of adventure, which are the very hallmarks of our witness, must somehow be woven through our careful considerations. Although we can expect to be uncomfortable at the prospect of being challenged and transformed through the travelling ministry, we can also fully celebrate the beginning, the journey itself and its completion.

New energy

Working at these elements *together*, in our various meetings seems to be vital. Dina van Dalfsen, a Dutch Friend who died in 1993, threw a challenge to Friends in Europe by leaving a legacy under the collective care of Netherlands, German and Britain Yearly Meetings, Belgium and Luxembourg Monthly Meeting and the Europe and Middle East Section of FWCC.

Dina's condition was that the beneficiaries combine to organise an event on *"the spiritual strengths and capacities of Quakers, now and in the past; in which ways these could be enhanced and applied to all human beings in general and to promote peace and reconciliation in particular, paying attention to modern research in the field of para-normal or psychic faculties"*.

A process in which as many European Friends as possible can be involved is envisaged. In this way, it is hoped to "bring about revival and rejuvenation of our Quaker identity and witness". From a preparatory conference in February 1997, came new energy and vision for a 'vibrant Quaker society'. Participants from the above meetings, with the addition of Ireland and Switzerland, saw that making full use of a travelling and teaching ministry had a key part to play in the development of trust, confidence and listening, which enables us to move outwards in the world, speaking our truth and hearing that of others.

Travelling under concern …. with a message

Although being careful not to elevate the travelling ministry to an unattainable height, I think that we would be wrong to underestimate the potential it has. Perhaps we need to 're-discover' and use it, describing it for what it is.

Ursula Windsor recalls that the German for 'travelling in the ministry' is 'Botschaftsreise', literally meaning *'travelling with a message'*. She goes on to say that *"in English, ministry can have so many facets, so that the purpose of 'travelling ministry', in its strict meaning, is lost."*

Clarity and agreement on what we mean by it would help us considerably. From interactions with many Friends, I have the sense that we should use the term, *travel under concern*, to describe the activity.

Love as the first motion

Whilst travelling...in friendship...and visiting Quakers in other lands, the importance of the two greatest commandments have come home to me – again and again – very strongly. The first – to love God with all my heart, soul and mind leads me to accept that God also loves me. Through the second – to love myself and my friends, family, workmates, companions in worship, neighbours –I can see the practical application of God's love. Although it is not easy and I continue to fail, I have recognised that my own strength alone is almost nothing. In fact, I no longer trust it. If I am to achieve anything worthwhile, I must wait for additional strength, from God.

In the conclusion of her presidential address to the Friends Historical Society in 1964, Elfrida Vipont Foulds uses the following words, which also seem to be a fitting end to this booklet.

"*Like all work done in God's name, travel under concern is deeply sacramental. John Woolman* (writing in his Journal) *gives us the key to it. 'Love was the first motion, and thence the concern arose'. It is the outward and visible sign of the inward and spiritual grace, or it is nothing. It is because of this that the cost is so great. We love to take a quotation out of its context and talk about George Fox telling us to 'walk cheerfully over the world'. The full passage* (from The Journal of George Fox) *is too hard for us.*

'And this is the word of the Lord God to you all, and a charge to you all in the presence of the living God, be patterns, be examples in all countries, places, islands, nations, wherever you come; that your carriage and life may preach among all sorts of people, and to them. Then you will come to walk cheerfully over the world, answering that of God in every one; whereby in them ye may be a blessing, and make the witness of God in them to bless you.'

There is only one source from which we can draw strength for such an undertaking as travel under concern, only one source which will enable us to walk cheerfully over the world. It is a source which has never failed. 'Have not I commanded thee? Be strong and of good courage; be not afraid, neither be thou dismayed: for the Lord thy God is with thee withersoever thou goest' (Joshua, chap.1, v.9) ".

APPENDIX A

Suggested responsibilities for those travelling under concern

In addition to spiritual preparation for the visit, attention to the following may also be important:-

1) Find out as much as possible about the meetings you intend to visit, including the forms and practices of the traditions out of which they arise. Be able to present a picture of the world family of Friends that includes and embraces them.

2) Be careful not to be a burden on your hosts.

3) Avoid 'preaching at' your expected audience by using presentation methods which encourage participation from those gathered.

4) Be open to meet with all sizes of groups, families and individuals over a sufficient period of time to gain a valid sense of the special strengths, needs, problems or opportunities of these Friends.

5) Be prepared to listen – sensitively – to ideas, problems or tensions being experienced by the worshipping community. Avoid taking sides or appearing to have all the answers.

6) At all times, respect confidentiality.

7) Be able and prepared to share deeply from your own religious life and experience. State your convictions in ways that will invite others to do the same.

8) Well in advance, inform those responsible for making arrangements for your visit of any special physical or dietary needs or limitations you may have. Also, indicate any personal interests you would like to pursue if time permits.

9) Send material about yourself that can be used for publicity purposes together with a list of topics you are prepared to discuss. Say in advance if you will need any particular equipment such as slide projector etc.

10) Make transport arrangements ahead of time.

11) Develop a broad outline of your planned itinerary, with dates, venues, aims and objectives.

12) As soon as possible after your visit, send a letter of thanks to the hosting meeting (and a written report to the appropriate body if one is specifically asked for).

13) Keep a full account of your expenses for future reference or claiming from Trusts, meetings etc.

Suggested responsibilities of local meetings

Hosts should not feel that they have to make elaborate or luxurious arrangements. All a visitor needs is genuine, friendly and considerate hospitality. However, it is helpful to:-

1) Provide the visitor with a room and a bed which he/she does not have to share with other persons or family pets.

2) Allow ample private time for the visitor to rest, write, do laundry, prepare for meetings etc.

3) Offer the opportunity to worship with the family or local group.

4) Offer – but not insist – to show the visitor local points of interest.

5) Protect the visitor from feeling obliged to over-eat (some feel they give offence if every dish isn't sampled or the offer of second helpings taken up).

6) Provide the visitor with a detailed description of the plans for the visit, including times, places, subjects of meetings and the names of key people the visitor will meet. Discuss programmes with them.

7) Prepare thoroughly for the visit so that best use can be made of the visitor and the topic.

8) Be aware of transport needs and plan accordingly.

9) Think of the possibility of contributing towards the visitor's travel expenses.

10) Delegate tasks – such as opening the meeting house, hosting a social evening, food preparation, overnight accommodation, clerking a meeting, driving etc to as many members of the meeting as possible.

11) If specifically asked for, send a report of the visit to the appropriate body. Suggestions for improving future visits can be included.

Adapted from FWCC Section of the Americas Guidelines for arranging visitations.

APPENDIX B

Useful addresses

Cuban Quaker Project: Eduardo Diaz, 13625 SW 82nd CT, Miami, Fl 33158, USA.

Directory for Travelling Friends: Friends General Conference, 1216 Arch Street, 2B, Philadelphia, PA, 19017, USA.

Earlham School of Religion, 228 College Ave., Richmond, IN 47374, USA.

Friends World Committee for Consultation:
World Office: 4 Byng Place, London WC1E 7JH, UK.
Section of the Americas: 1506 Race Street, Philadelphia, PA, 19102, USA.
Latin American Program (COAL): Guerrero No 223 Pte, Zona Centro Cd. Mante TAM., 89800 Mexico.
Asia-West Pacific Section: 657 Mount Eden Road, Auckland 4, Aotearoa/New Zealand.
Europe & Middle East Section: PO Box 808, AV Leiden, The Netherlands.
Africa Section: PO Box 41946, Friends International Centre, N'gong Road, Nairobi, Kenya.

George Fox College, Newberg, Oregon, OR 97132, USA. Tel: (503) 538 8383.

Bosse Karlberg, photographer of art and writer; Polgatan 8c, 21611 Malmö, Sweden. Tel: +46.40.161084.

New Foundation Fellowship: UK Enquiries to Godwin Arnold, 97 Northcourt Avenue, Reading RG2 7HG. Tel: +44 (0)1743 874204.

Northern Friends Peace Board: Victoria Hall, Knowsley Street, Bolton BL1 2AS, UK. Tel: +44 (0)1204 382330. E-mail: nfpb@gn.apc.org.

Pendle Hill Quaker Center: 338 Plush Mill Road, Wallingford, PA 19086-6099, USA.

Quaker Bolivia Link: Ken & Pam Barratt, 12 Redcote Road, South Parade, West Kirby, Wirral L48 0RR, UK.

Quaker Friends of Cuba: Marigold Best, 19 Buckingham Street, Oxford OX1 4LH, UK.

Quaker Home Service: Friends House, 173-177 Euston Road, London NW1 2BJ, UK. Tel: +44 (0)171 387 3601.

Sessions of York/The Ebor Press: York YO3 9HS, UK. Tel: +44 (0)1904 659224.

The Joseph Rowntree Charitable Trust: The Garden House, Water End, York YO3 6LP, UK. Tel: +44 (0)1904 627810. E-mail: jrct@gn.apc.org.

Wider Quaker Fellowship: a program of the FWCC, Section of the Americas (see address under FWCC).

Woodbrooke College: 1046 Bristol Road, Birmingham B29 6LJ, UK. Tel: +44 (0)121 472 5171; Fax: +44 (0)121 472 5173.

REFERENCE SOURCES

Ambler, Rex: *The Discipline of Light*; paper to the Quaker Theology Seminar 1996.

Ambler, Rex: *Experiment with Light*; paper, March 1996.

Ambler, Rex: *Quaker Identity-anything goes?*; paper, April 1996.

Auckland Friends Prayer Support Group: *Visiting under Concern*; 1987.

Barbour, Hugh: *The Quakers in Puritan England*; Friends United Press, 1964.

Barnes, Irwin & Sylvia: *Windows:looking at ecumenical issues*; 1993.

Braithwaite, William C: *The Beginnings of Quakerism*; reprinted 1981 JRCT and Sessions of York, England.

Braithwaite, William C: *The Second Period of Quakerism*; reprinted 1979 JRCT and Sessions of York, England.

Brayshaw, A. Neave: *The Quakers: their story and message*; reprinted 1982 Sessions of York, England.

Browne, Gordon M. Jr: *The Future of Quakerism*; Wider Quaker Fellowship, 1967.

Christian Faith & Practice; London Yearly Meeting,1960.

Edwards, Jeni: *The Flight of the Bumblebee*; Bumblebee Booklets, 1994.

Faith & Practice; N. Pacific Yearly Meeting, 1986.

Faith in Action: Encounters with Friends; FWCC and Sessions of York, 1991.

Ferguson, Val: *Carrying the Quaker message today*; Wider Quaker Fellowship, 1988.

Fernandez, Loida: *Travelling along the Central America Bridge*; July 1996 (report).

Fryer, Jonathan: *George Fox and the Children of the Light*; Kyle Cathie Ltd., 1991.

Foulds, Elfrida Vipont: *Travel under Concern*; Journal of FHS Vol. 50, No. 4, 1964.

Greenwood, Ormerod (text): *The Quaker Tapestry*; Impact Books, 1990.

Heron, Alastair: *The Quakers: yesterday, today and tomorrow*; Quaker Outreach Yorkshire, 1992.

Hoare, Edward: *Deepening the Spiritual Life of the Meeting*; Friends General Conference, 1995.

Hoare, Edward: *A Role for the Travelling Friend*; *The Friend*, 10th January 1986.

Hoare, Edward: *Reflections of a Travelling Friend*; *The Friend*, 19th January 1990.

Hoare, Edward: *Being Present for Another*; *The Friend*, 18th May 1990.

Hoare, Edward: *Travelling in the Ministry – a report for The J. R. Charitable Trust*, 1992.

Hobday, Teresa: *My Ministry*; September 1993 (unpublished).

Hobday, Teresa: *The Ministerial Needs of the Unprogrammed Tradition*; 1994 (unpublished).

Hope Bacon, Margaret: *The Quiet Rebels*; New Society Publishers, 1985.

Jones, Rufus: *Later Periods of Quakerism, Vols 1 & 2*; Macmillan & Co., 1921.

Journal of John Woolman and a plea for the poor; Citadel Press Inc., 1961.

Meeting the Spirit; FWCC-EMES, 1995.

Northern Friends Peace Board Annual Reports 1993-95; Travelling in the listening ministry 1993-95 (paper).

Peck, George T: *What is Quakerism? A Primer...*; Pendle Hill 277.

Pulford, David: *Warm Kettles and a Cold Flannel: Report on Intervisitation in Botswana, Lesotho and South Africa 1995-6*; Quaker Peace Centre, 1996.

Punshon, John: *Portrait in Grey......*; Quaker Home Service, 1984.

Quaker Faith & Practice; Britain Yearly Meeting, 1995.

Santos, Heredio: *A Bridge of Love*; Wider Quaker Fellowship, 1993.

Sharman, Cecil W: *George Fox and the Quakers*; Quaker Home Service/Friends United Press, 1991.

Watson, George H: *A Handbook on Travelling under Religious Concern*; FWCC, 1986 (unpublished).

Windsor, Ursula: *Prophetic Quakerism & Vocational Ministry in the Society of Friends*; Friends Quarterly, July 1996.

Wood, Duncan: *The People called Quakers*; FWCC Europe and Near East Section.